LANDLINE
CUBED   SS, 15

SEAN SCULLY

CHEIM & READ

Five Thoughts After Sean Scully
Pac Pobric

It is striking how often, in the literature on Sean Scully, memory emerges as the key to the discussion. "His sense of art, the seemingly obsolete act of communicating meaning by smearing mud on cloth, is anchored in the past."[1] Robert Hughes wrote this of Scully in 1989 and who could say otherwise? Scully is a traditionalist, and traditions, more than anything else, are about not forgetting, even as one is inventing anew. The most cursory glance at his painting yields this: that the Cubist grid, now more than 100 years old, sits beneath each work; that Kazimir Malevich and Paul Klee are remembered in his style; and that Diego Velázquez, with his soft edge and muted color, has been Scully's most enduring teacher, the one artist whose lessons he most fully absorbed. (Rothko, contrary to Scully orthodoxy, was only the intermediary.)

Yet memory is so often faulty, or at least selective, and as I write this, I am having trouble recalling *Stack*, 2016, a sculpture by Scully that's set outside his studio in Tappan, New York. I first saw it in a photograph that gave a skewed impression that quickly dissipated when I saw it in person maybe three weeks later. Up close, it was wider than I imagined, and made not of solid slabs of metal, but open frames, like those for pictures, piled one atop another. I knew already that the frames varied in dimension, so that some jutted out while others receded, but I did not expect it to be so forbidding, as if it wanted to keep me at bay. I said to Scully as we walked around it that it was imposing, because it was. Looking back at the photograph, with dimensions appended, I'm reminded why: it's fifteen feet tall.

I asked him about the metal. What kind was it? Bronze, perhaps, or painted aluminum? Tony Smith came to mind, I said. But no, it was weathering steel, Scully told me, pointing across the yard to another work, *Boxes of Air*, 2015, made of the same Corten alloy. The two works, especially in close proximity, looked radically dissimilar. *Stack* is closed from most perspectives, as if it were peering inward, and its black shell is severe and protective; *Boxes of Air* is made differently, of open rectangular cubes that frame the landscape, and it is softened by its copper patina. But one day, Scully said, in probably a year's time, *Stack* would anneal to the same dusty brown that tempers the neighboring sculpture.

Weathering steel is a contingent material. It rusts more quickly in some environments than others. In areas where dampness is persistent, corrosion can become a problem. But the steel is relatively impermeable, and with minimal maintenance, it is designed to withstand harsh conditions for extended periods. I did not know this when I first saw *Stack*, and the knowledge now obscures—even spoils—my diminished recollection. Who knows precisely how it will age? And anyway, it may already look differently than when I saw it those weeks ago. Will it even be the same sculpture once it fully rusts? Perhaps one day it will much more closely resemble *Boxes of Air*, but I cannot say for sure. In hindsight, I am glad *Stack* is not so vivid because every day it is a changed work, and memory serves poorly here.

■ ■ ■

At the time of my visit to Tappan late last year, Scully was in the process of fabricating another version of *Stack* for this show, but other new works were already finished. He was eager to show them. We looked at watercolors on paper, a marble sculpture, oil stick drawings, and aluminum paintings, all of which he was comfortable describing, as if he had been looking at them for years.

He was at ease, too, in drawing connections, which was perhaps my first impression of him. The first time we met, in his former studio in Manhattan, I was struck by his itinerant mind and the James Joycean quality of his speech. He was deeply concerned with communication, he told me ("I am not a reticent person"), and he was continuously in the midst of building one bridge or another between ideas. I found it difficult to slow him down, which was charming and mildly bewildering. How was it that everything he said came out as already considered when he seemed to be improvising this whole time? I suppose it has to do with his experience navigating journalists, because later I recognized the same skillful mind at work when I read his measured response to a writer who asked whether his work was simply a repetitive exploitation of Robert Motherwell's own stripe painting, *Little Spanish Prison* from 1941–44. Scully said: "The painting is fantastic, great, one of his best paintings. But there is a difference between implication and achievement . . . He did his little painting. What I have done, historically, is to explode the possibilities of it."[2]

The writer's question was ill-informed; Motherwell, in truth, is far from Scully. His *Little Spanish Prison* is only superficially related to the stripes we know, which Scully in fact distilled through a counterintuitive sort of formal magic from Matisse, and especially his Moroccan paintings from 1912–13. Motherwell, anyway, did not have the patience to follow through on his picture, which remains in his oeuvre as a beautiful aberration, whereas Scully has nothing but patience for stripes.

Yet I have always admired Scully's diplomatic, if self-serving, phrasing—how evocative the explosion that shatters that prison!—because it works on a figurative level to illuminate his ambivalence. His pictures are attached, formally and discursively, to a Modernist tradition to which he is chained by a pair of golden handcuffs. He is welcome to luxuriate in the glow of abstraction, but his wandering is limited, and any path he should choose is circumscribed by what he has inherited. Restriction can be liberating—it allows for focus, and Scully's art in particular has benefited from the trimmed narrative it fits into—but the weight of inheritance is heavy. Of Malevich's *Black Square*, 1915, he once told me that only "a social cataclysm" (he meant the 20th century) could prompt such a work. He added: "You can't make an abstract painting after that that doesn't have a precedent. It's impossible." He meant it as a lament and a reprieve.

■ ■ ■

Some days ago, in trying to puzzle out a riddle about abstraction, I came upon this passage from Saint Augustine: "With regard to the past, when this is reported correctly what is brought out from the memory is not the events themselves (these are already past) but words conceived from the images of those events, which, in passing through the senses, have left as it were their footprints stamped upon the mind."[3]

The riddle was this: how is it that pictures of nothing accumulate meaning? Because if you look at abstract painting—Malevich's or Rothko's, or even Klee's grid pictures—what resonates most is its emptiness. "With illusionism," Kirk Varnedoe offered in 2006, "the argument could be made that art progressed by a series of corrections, made according to the unchanging standard of nature and perceptual mechanics." But these were only conventions, now long gone, and the new ones are "dumb, man-made forms like cubes, stripes, and other architectural configurations."[4] (He was not thinking of Scully, but he could have been.)

Earlier Modernists sensed the problem clearly and postured defensively to make up for the lack. "There is no such thing as a good painting about nothing," Rothko said in a 1943 statement published by the *New York Times* (it was co-written by Adolph Gottlieb and Barnett Newman).[5] But such talk does not inhere in a picture of blurred stacks of orange and yellow; it comes from outside the painting and motivates it, but does not explain it. It is the same with Scully's work. The five watercolor columns in *Blue Note 9.16*, 2016, say nothing on their own. Similar works, like *Wall Of Light Cubed 9.16.15*, 2015, and *Wall Of Light Cubed 9.25.15*, 2015, are titled with dates, which foregrounds their quietude. Arthur Danto once wrote anxiously of Scully that his works are "abstract paintings, but flooded with meaning" and he allowed the uncertainty of that "but" to hang and ring.

The problem is deepened, not resolved, when a work is titled to make clear reference to something outside itself. The names of three paintings Scully did in the 1980s—*Molloy*, 1984, *Pale Fire*, 1988, and *Heart of Darkness*, 1982—do indeed recall books by Samuel Beckett, Vladimir Nabokov, and Joseph Conrad, but recollection is not depiction. How could a stripe ever describe a novel? The thought is unsustainable and the rift between the paintings and the words grows wider.

Augustine's remark, kidnapped from his intended context, offers some solution: it is memory—imprinted by language and related to new experience—that makes for meaning. This is how tradition builds: by describing what is new in terms of what is old and thereby enlivening both. Scully's call to Beckett and Nabokov and Conrad is not a matter of representation; instead, he seeks connection to a language he cherishes. (Thinking back, this must explain his elegant and expansive manner of speaking, which so richly evokes a Modern—especially Irish—literary tradition.)

The finest critics, too, demonstrate that the real meaning of his work emerges in the memories his art enriches. Thus Robert Hughes made this insightful and elegant comparison by drawing on his wealth of experience: "You can see the traces of [Scully's] idols throughout the work: especially, in his liking for silvery grays, pinks, and a constant regulating black, Velázquez, the greatest 'impersonal' painter who ever lived."[6]

To get from Velázquez to Scully at maturity, much is lost—the figure, deep recessive space, all sense of external subject matter—but what remained, for Hughes, was Scully's taste for soft edges and a muted palette ("silvery grays" is an especially fine description). Try to imagine Scully without Velázquez; what do you see? Picture his work without Cubism or Malevich or Klee: it could exist, maybe, but its lack of precedent would make it meaningless, even invisible. Scully once called relationships "the problem of the world" that his art was meant to solve, but a painting can only harbor such ambition through the connections we make when looking and

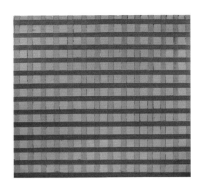

Crossover Painting 1, 1974,
acrylic on canvas,
102 x 108 in, 259 x 274.3 cm

speaking and writing.[7] This is why we rarely ever see a picture in a room by itself. Art matters only relatively, especially abstract art. Looking back on my visit to Tappan, I now understand why Scully insisted on pulling out each of his oil stick drawings before presenting them to me as a group. They look better in a row, don't they? he asked. They did, but I wasn't sure why. It is clearer to me now—self-evident, even. Yet I cannot abide by Augustine's other belief: that new thoughts that appear obvious are assemblages of old memories, things forgotten after the fall and brought back with new experience. I admire the idealism of his Platonism, but it is impossible to believe today. The photographs (what are they but memories?) I now have of Scully's work don't rehearse my experience in Tappan as it really was, even if they do encourage the words that recollect it.

∎ ∎ ∎

I once told Scully I thought of immigration as a beautiful metaphor for the difficulty of maintaining tradition. You are born in a place and you acquire its habits and customs and tastes, and then you leave, and what happens to that past? It is not impossible to hold onto—some practices follow despite an immigrant's conscious intentions—but an old life cannot be lived just the same way in a new place. The pressure or desire to retain can be strong, but the need to adapt is inexorably stronger. Transformation is inevitable.

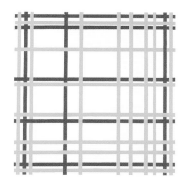

Piet Mondrian, New York City I,
1942, oil on canvas,
47 x 45 in, 119.3 x 114.2 cm

The thought came back to me when I came across a reproduction of Scully's 1974 work *Crossover Painting 1*, which bears remarkable likeness to Piet Mondrian's *New York City I*, 1942, done two years after the Dutch artist fled the war for Manhattan. Look at the Mondrian picture and you will know it is his, but resettlement has deeply shaken his style. It is not simply that the lines in the painting are not black, but colored; it is also that, for the first time since he adopted his signature flat format in 1920, depth has been aggressively reasserted. The red, yellow, and blue stripes that cross the canvas are woven: red is atop yellow at some meetings and below it at others, and blue courses beneath the other two colors at each crossing, except one, where it overruns yellow.

Mondrian had a genuinely conservative personality; it was imbued by his Calvinist upbringing. He had no desire to create rupture. But how could his work not change now that he was in the New World? To adapt, he absorbed the world around him and focused. Watching Mondrian repeatedly reconfigure his final, unfinished work, *Victory Boogie-Woogie*, 1944, his friend Carl Holty asked why he didn't simply make numerous works with various solutions. Mondrian replied: "I don't want pictures. I just want to find things out."[8]

In my office, looking over my catalogues of Scully's work, it occurs to me that he, too, has let go of so much since his emigration to New York from London in 1975. The stripes he realized in an

Untitled (Homage to Paul Klee), 1968,
gouache on cardstock,
5 3/4 x 8 in, 14.6 x 20.3 cm

Figure on Chair, 1964,
pencil on paper,
22 x 15 in, 55.9 x 37.8 cm

untitled homage to Paul Klee from 1968 are still in his pictures, but the bright, cheery openness of the Swiss-German artist is gone. Portraits of sitters from 1966–67 closely resemble his recent paintings of his son, Oisín (to whom he has dedicated a painting cycle), but the charm of small oil pastels on paper is no longer enough; now it is large gestures on aluminum. And from a remarkable and anomalous drawing of a suited man in a chair (through which Scully finally assimilated Cubism in 1964), nothing remains in his recent work but the structural scaffold and the condensed perspective.

In speaking to Scully about immigration, I mentioned my own move to the United States from Sarajevo when I was four. It was not difficult for me; I was just a child. I have always considered myself American, I told him, and he nodded and said he was around the same age when he emigrated from Ireland to England. He became English in a similar sense after his move—ninety-eight percent so, he said. "But the two percent—that's incurable."

■ ■ ■

Today, I have learned something new about weathering steel: underneath the rust it will form, some trace of the former black, given the proper care, will always remain.

For Mom, and Dad

Untitled, 1966–67,
oil pastel on paper,
8 × 8 in. 20.7 × 20.4 cm

Oisín on the Beach, 2016,
oil on aluminum,
85 × 75 in. 215.9 × 190.5 cm

[1] Robert Hughes, *Nothing If Not Critical* (New York: Penguin, 1990), 349.

[2] Quoted in Victoria Combalia, "Sean Scully: Against Formalism," in *Sean Scully: Twenty Years*, 1976–1995, ed. Ned Rifkin (Atlanta: High Museum of Art, 1995), 33.

[3] Saint Augustine, *Confessions*, quoted in *The Human Experience of Time*, ed. Charles M. Sherover (New York: New York University Press, 1985), 86.

[4] Kirk Varnedoe, *Pictures of Nothing* (Princeton: Princeton University Press, 2006), 29.

[5] Quoted in Edward Alden Jewell, "'Globalism' Pops into View," *New York Times*, June 13, 1943, 9.

[6] Hughes, 349.

[7] Scully quoted in *Sean Scully: Painting*, https://www.youtubecomwatch?v=LWMqrNIdBRk.

[8] Quoted in Yve-Alain Bois, *Painting as Model* (Cambridge: MIT Press, 1993), 183.

Landline Blue Haze, 2016, oil on aluminum, 85 × 75 in, 215.9 × 190.5 cm

Doric Pale Blue, 2016, oil on copper, 24 x 27 1/2 in, 61 x 69.9 cm

Wall of Light Cubed 9.25.15, 2015, watercolor on paper, 30 × 22 1/4 in, 76.2 × 56.5 cm

WALL OF LIGHT CUBED   Sean Scully 9.25.15

Block Red, 2016, oil on aluminum, 85 x 75 in, 215.9 x 190.5 cm

Wall of Light Cubed 9.16.15, 2015, watercolor on paper, 22 1/4 x 30 in, 56.5 x 76.2 cm

Ten Ton Ceiling, 2017, bronze and stainless steel, 34 x 70 x 47 in, 86.4 x 177.8 x 119.4 cm

Doric 9.20.16, 2016, pastel on paper, 40 x 60 in, 101.6 x 152.4 cm

Block Brown, 2016, oil on aluminum, 85 × 75 in, 215.9 × 190.5 cm

Brown Silver Tower, 2016, Corten and stainless steel, 108 × 36 × 36 in, 274.3 × 91.4 × 91.4 cm
Doric Pale Blue, 2016, oil on copper, 24 × 28 in, 61 × 71.1 cm

Blue Note 9.16, 2016, watercolor on paper, 22 x 30 1/4 in, 55.9 x 76.8 cm

ONE NOTE   Sean Scully '86

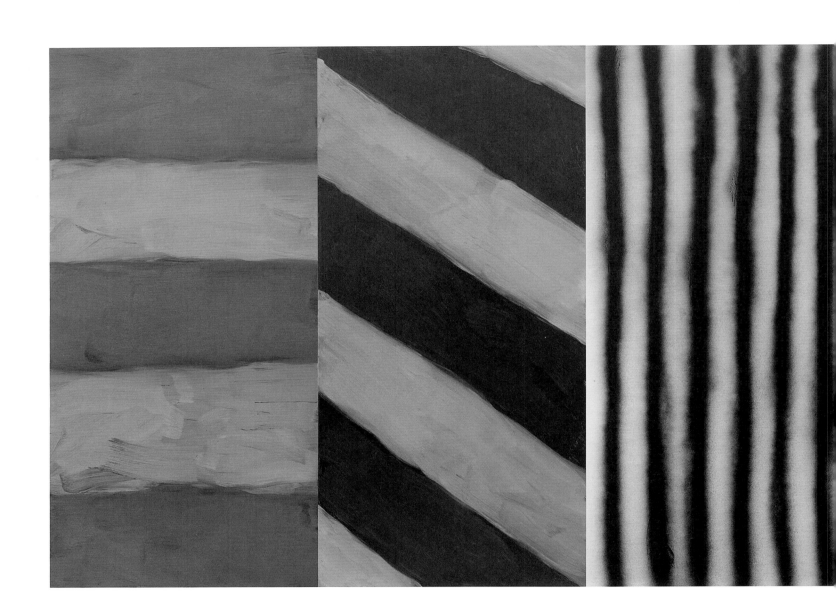

Blue Note, 2016, oil and acrylic spray on aluminum, 110 × 320 in, 279.4 × 812.8 cm

Stack 2, 2016, watercolor and graphite on paper, 22 x 30 1/4 in, 55.9 x 76.8 cm

Colored Stacked Frames, 2017, stainless steel with automotive paint, 10 × 8 × 8 ft, 3 × 2.4 × 2.4 m

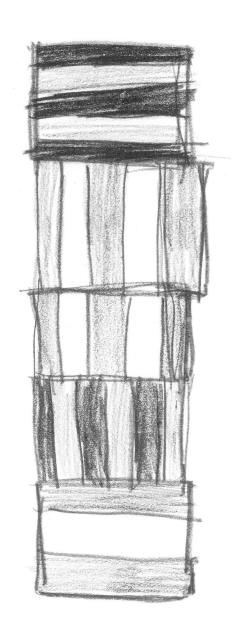

SS 82

A chronology of the sculpture

Crann Soilse, 2003, Chinese black basalt and Portuguese limestone, 10 1/2 × 105 × 8 ft, 3.2 × 32 × 2.4 m
University of Limerick, Limerick, Ireland

SCULLY
MOOSEURACH
82549 KONIGSDORF
GERMANY

Nov 8·07

Thinking about about the stone block.
Thinking about the wall of light cubed,
which stands in a field near Aix.
When I saw in the stone yard in Portugal,
I could only think of two things: one was
Jackson Pollock and the other was
Finnegans Wake by Joyce. Both are
non - negotiable, both crowd out, or crowd
space, Pollock with a dizzying visual
attack, and Joyce with characters and
narrative that confuses the space and
time, that could be used to make a
narrative and nearly doesnt. I was
thinking, standing in front of my sculpture that
it was the unnegotiating squeezing of space
out of sculpture. Compression as a force.
     From afar it looks like a giant
painting, and from near - organized
rubble.
     If in the future someone from another
cultural matrix, who doesnt value my

cultural matrix, takes off a stone or two or three, to build something else – it will still survive. Its compressing stubborness will still hold it together. It pushes in, and what you cannot see, you can feel. You know it is cubed. You know that, in fact, a true argument, is stronger than an appearance!

When you look at a tree, you are looking at the outside knowing the inside, when you look at a rock or the sea, you look at the outside knowing the inside. Seeing and knowing are involved in this work, in what it is. And if some of it, is taken away, it will still be what it is,

Wall of Light Cubed, 2007, granite, 13 × 65 × 26 ft, 4 × 20 × 8 m
Château La Coste, Le Puy Ste Réparade, France

Tower, 2009, stone maquette, 29 1/2 × 8 × 8 in, 74.9 × 20.3 × 20.3 cm

China Piled-Up, 2014, Corten steel, 12 × 50 × 20 ft, 3.6 × 15.2 × 6.1 m

Shanghai Himalayas Museum, Shanghai

Boxes of Air (after Seamus Heaney), 2015, Corten steel, 12 × 50 × 20 ft, 3.7 × 15.2 × 6.1 m
Château La Coste, Le Puy Ste Réparade, France

Untitled (Tower), 2015, Corten steel, 108 × 36 × 36 in, 274.3 × 91.4 × 91.4 cm

Landline Cubed, 2015, stainless steel, 108 x 36 x 36 in, 274.3 x 91.4 x 91.4 cm

Untitled (Tower), 2015, marble, 96 x 24 x 24 in, 243.8 x 61 x 61 cm

Stack, 2016, Corten steel, 15 × 12 × 12 ft, 4.5 × 3.6 × 3.6 m

BIOGRAPHY

Born 1945 Dublin
1962–1965   The Central School of Art, London
1965–1968   Croydon College of Art, London
1968–1972   Bachelor of Arts, Newcastle University, England
Lives and works in New York and Munich

SOLO EXHIBITIONS

2017
Sean Scully: *Wall of Light Cubed*, Cheim & Read, New York
Sean Scully, Kunsthaus Lempertz, Brussels, Belgium
Sean Scully, Multimedia Art Museum, Moscow

2016
Sean Scully: *Circa 70*, Cheim & Read, Ridgewood, Queens, New York
Sean Scully: *Resistance and Persistence*, curated by Philip Dodd, Ingleby Gallery, Edinburgh,
Scotland; traveled to Art Museum of the Nanjing University of the Arts, Nanjing, China;
Guangdong Museum of Art, Guangzhou, China; Hubei Museum of Art, Wuhan, China
Sean Scully: *The Body and the Frame,* Dům Umění České Budějovice, House of Art, Budweis, Czech Republic
Sean Scully: *The Eighties*, Mnuchin Gallery, New York
Sean Scully. *BOOK*, Garrison Art Center, The Riverside Galleries, Garrison, New York
Sean Scully: *Metal*, Galerie Lelong, Paris
Sean Scully: *Horizon*, Timothy Taylor Gallery, London

2015
Sean Scully: *Landline*, Cheim & Read, New York
Sean Scully: *Moving or Profound or Necessary or Beautiful, 1974–2015*, Pinacoteca do Estado and
Centro Universitário Maria Antonia, São Paulo, Brazil
Sean Scully: *Painting as an imaginative world appropriation*, Museum Liaunig, Neuhas, Austria
Sean Scully: *Land Sea*, La Biennale di Venezia 'Collateral Events,' Palazzo Falier, Venice, Italy
Sean Scully, National Gallery of Ireland, Dublin
Sean Scully: *Home*, Kerlin Gallery, Dublin
Sean Scully: *Sta. Cecilia*, Church of Sta. Cecilia, Barcelona
Sean Scully: *Different Places*, Château La Coste, Le Puy-Sainte-Réparade, France
Sean Scully: *Four Days*, Galerie Michael Kewenig, Berlin

2014

Sean Scully: Doric, Galerie Lelong, Paris
Sean Scully: A New Master Among Old Masters, Christ Church Picture Gallery, Oxford, England
Sean Scully: Kind of Red, Timothy Taylor Gallery, London
Sean Scully: Figure/Abstract, Ludwig Museum, Koblenz, Germany; traveled to Kunsthalle Rostock, Rostock, Germany; Crawford Art Gallery, Cork, Ireland
Sean Scully, Galerie Klüser & Galerie Klüser 2, Munich, Germany
Sean Scully: Follow the Heart, Shanghai Himalayas Museum, Shanghai; traveled to Central Academy of Fine Art, Beijing

2013

Sean Scully: Night and Day, Cheim & Read, New York
Sean Scully: Triptychs, Pallant House Gallery, Chichester, West Sussex, England

2012

Sean Scully: Works on Paper / Wall of Light Red Shade, Van Every / Smith Galleries, Davidson College, Davidson, North Carolina
Sean Scully: Change and Horizontals, curated by Brett Littman and Joanna Kleinberg, Timothy Taylor Gallery, London; traveled to Middlesbrough Institute of Modern Art, Middlesbrough, England; Walter Storms Galerie, Munich, Germany; Galleria nazionale d'arte moderna e contemporanea, Rome; The Drawing Center, New York
Sean Scully: Grey Wolf – A Retrospective, curated by Annick Haldemann and Brigitte Reutner, Kunstmuseum Bern, Switzerland; traveled to Lentos Kunstmuseum, Linz, Austria
Sean Scully: Luz del Sur, Alhambra – Palacio Carlos V, Granada, Spain
Sean Scully: Doric, Benaki Museum of Art, Athens, Greece; traveled to Institut Valencià d'Art Modern (IVAM), Valencia, Spain; Dublin City Gallery The Hugh Lane, Dublin; Musée d'Art Classique de Mougins, Mougins, France
Sean Scully, The Verey Gallery, Eton College, Windsor, England
Sean Scully: The Evocative Capacity of Painting, Wooson Gallery, Daegu, South Korea
Notations: Sean Scully, Philadelphia Museum of Art, Pennsylvania

2011

Sean Scully: Works from the 1980s, Wilhelm-Hack Museum, Ludwigshafen, Germany
Sean Scully: Works on Paper, Luther W. Brady Art Gallery, George Washington University, Washington, D.C.
Sean Scully: Cut Ground, Kerlin Gallery, Dublin
Sean Scully: Paintings and Watercolors, Chazen Museum of Art, University of Wisconsin Madison, Madison, Wisconsin

2010

Sean Scully: Works from the 1980s, curated by Tanja Pirsig Marshall, VISUAL – Centre for Contemporary Art, Carlow, Ireland; traveled to Leeds Art Gallery, Leeds, England

Sean Scully: Works from the Modern Art Museum of Fort Worth, The Old Jail Art Center, Albany, Texas
Sean Scully: Iona, Ingleby Gallery, Edinburgh, Scotland
Sean Scully: New Work, Timothy Taylor Gallery, London
Die Bilderwelt von Sean Scully, Kunstsammlungen Chemnitz, Chemnitz, Germany
Sean Scully: Liliane, Alexander and Bonin, New York

2009
Sean Scully: Paintings from the 80's, Timothy Taylor Gallery, London
Constantinople or the Sensual Concealed: The Imagery of Sean Scully, curated by Susanne Kleine, Museum Küppersmühle für Moderne Kunst, Duisburg, Germany; traveled to Ulster Museum, Belfast, Northern Ireland
Sean Scully: Recent Works, Walter Storms Galerie, Munich
Sean Scully: Emotion and Structure, House of Fine Arts / Modern Gallery – László Vass Collection, Veszprém, Hungary
Sean Scully: Recent Paintings, Galerie Lelong, New York

2008
Sean Scully: The Art of the Stripe, Hood Museum of Art, Dartmouth College, Hanover, New Hampshire
Sean Scully: La surface peinte, Galerie Lelong, Paris
Sean Scully, Galeria Carles Taché, Barcelona

2007
Sean Scully: Dedicate a García Lorca, Instituto Cervantes Dublin, Dublin
Sean Scully: A Retrospective, curated by Danilo Eccher, Fundació Joan Miró, Barcelona; traveled to Musée d'Arte Moderne, St. Etienne, France; Museo d'Arte Contemporanea di Roma al Mattatoio, Rome
Sean Scully: Walls of Aran, Kerlin Gallery, Dublin
Sean Scully: Aran Islands: A Portfolio of Photographs, Galerie Lelong, New York
Sean Scully: Walls of Aran, Ingleby Gallery, Edinburgh, Scotland
The Prints of Sean Scully, curated by Joann Moser, Smithsonian American Art Museum, Washington, D.C.; traveled to Naples Museum of Art, Naples, Florida; Minneapolis Institute of Arts, Minneapolis, Minnesota; Hyde Collection, Glen Falls, New York
Sean Scully: New Painting, Galerie Jamileh Weber, Zürich

2006
Sean Scully: Die Architektur der Farbe / The Architecture of Color, Kunstmuseum Liechtenstein, Vaduz, Liechtenstein
Sean Scully, Bibliothèque Nationale de France, Paris
Sean Scully: Recent Paintings, L.A. Louver Gallery, Venice, California
Sean Scully, Timothy Taylor Gallery, London
Sean Scully, Scottish National Gallery of Modern Art, Edinburgh, Scotland

2005

Faith Hope Love, Augustinerkloster, Erfurt, Germany
Sean Scully: Graphic Works, Fenton Gallery, Cork, Ireland
Sean Scully: Paintings and Works on Paper, Abbot Hall Art Gallery at Lakeland Artists Trust, Kendal, England
Sean Scully: Malerie: kleine Formate, Staatliche Museen Kassel, Neue Galerie, Kassel, Germany
Sean Scully: New Work, Galerie Lelong, New York
Sean Scully, Ingleby Gallery, Edinburgh, Scotland
Mirrors 1982–2004 prints, editions & photographs, La Louviere Museum, La Louviere, Belgium
Sean Scully: Photographs, Galeria Carles Taché, Barcelona
Sean Scully: para García Lorca, La Sala de Exposiciones Acala 31, Madrid
Sean Scully: Wall of Light, curated by Stephen Phillips, Phillips Collection, Washington, D.C.; traveled to Modern Art Museum of Fort Worth, Fort Worth, Texas; Cincinnati Art Museum, Cincinnati, Ohio; Metropolitan Museum of Art, New York

2004

Sean Scully: Photographs, Galerie Bernd Klüser, Munich
Sean Scully, Kerlin Gallery, Dublin
Sean Scully: España-Spain-Spanien, Kunsthalle Weimar, Harry Graf Kessler, Weimar, Germany
Sean Scully: Fotografias, Galeria Estiarte, Madrid
Sean Scully: Winter Robe, Galerie Lelong, Paris
Sean Scully: Estampes 1983–2003, Centre Culturel Irlandais, Paris
Sean Scully: Paintings from the '70s, Timothy Taylor Gallery, London
tigres en el jardin: José Guerrero & Sean Scully, Centro José Guerrero, Granada, Spain
Sean Scully: Etchings for Federico García Lorca, Huerta de San Vicente, Casa-Museo Federico García Lorca Foundation, Granada, Spain
Holly Series, Kunstverein Aichach, Aichach, Germany
Sala de Dexposiciones de Caja de Duero, Palacio de Garcigrande, Salamanca, Spain
Sean Scully: Body of Light, National Gallery of Australia, Canberra, Australia
Sean Scully: Photographs, Anne Reed Gallery, Ketchum, Idaho

2003

Sean Scully, Hôtel des Arts, Toulon, France
Sean Scully, Galeria Carles Taché, Barcelona
Sean Scully: Photographs, Galerie Jamileh Weber, Zürich
Sean Scully: Works 1990–2003, Sara Hilden Art Museum, Tampere, Finland; traveled to Neues Museum Weimar, Weimar, Germany
Sean Scully: Photographs, L.A. Louver Gallery, Venice, California
Sean Scully: Prints and Photographs, Alexander and Bonin Gallery, New York
Sean Scully: Wall of Light, Figures, Timothy Taylor Gallery, London

2002

Sean Scully, Cámara de Comercio, Industria y Navegación de Cantabria, Santander, Spain; traveled to Ayuntamiento de Pamplona, Polvorín de la Cindadela, Spain

Sean Scully, Galerie Neue Meister, Staatliche Kunstsammlungen Dresden, Dresden, Germany

Sean Scully, L.A. Louver Gallery, Venice, California

Sean Scully: Wall of Light, Centro de Arte Helio Oiticica, Rio de Janeiro

2001

Barcelona Etchings for Federico García Lorca, Instituto Cervantes, London

Sean Scully: Light + Gravity: Recent Wall of Light Paintings, Knoedler & Company, New York

Sean Scully: New Works on Paper, Galerie Lelong, New York

Sean Scully: The 90s – Paintings, Pastels, Watercolors, Photographs, Kunstsammlung Nordrhein – Westfalen, Düsseldorf, Germany; traveled to Haus der Kunst, Munich, Germany; Institut Valencià d'Art Modern (IVAM), Valencia, Spain

Sean Scully: Work on Paper, Rex Irwin Gallery, Woollahra, Australia; traveled to Dickerson Gallery, Melbourne, Australia

Sean Scully, Ingleby Gallery, Edinburgh, Scotland

Sean Scully: Light to Dark, Galerie Lelong, Paris

Sean Scully: Walls, Windows, Horizons, David Winton Bell Gallery, List Art Center, Brown University, Providence, Rhode Island

Sean Scully, Musée Jenisch, Vevey, Switzerland

Sean Scully: Wall of Light, curated by Michael Auping, Museo De Arte Contemporaneo De Monterrey, Monterrey, Mexico; traveled to Museo de Arte Moderno, Mexico City, Mexico

2000

Sean Scully on Paper, Metropolitan Museum of Art, New York

Sean Scully: Prints 1994–1998, Alan Cristea Gallery, London

Sean Scully, Galeria Carles Taché, Barcelona

Sean Scully: Estampes 1983–1999, Musée des Beaux-Arts de Caen, Caen, France

Sean Scully: Photographies, Galerie de l'ancien collège, Ecole municipale d'arts plastiques, Châtellerault, France

Sean Scully: Graphics, A+A Galleria D'Arte, Venice, Italy

1999

Sean Scully, Galerie Lelong, Paris

Sean Scully: Prints 1968–1999, Graphische Sammlung Albertina, Vienna, Austria; traveled to Musée du Dessin et de l'Estampe Originale, Gravelines, France

Sean Scully: New Paintings and Works on Paper, Danese Gallery and Galerie Lelong, New York

Sean Scully: New Paintings, South London Gallery, London

Sean Scully: Monotypes and Color Woodcuts 1987–1993 from the Garner Tullis Workshop, Galerie Kornfeld, Zürich

Sean Scully, Kerlin Gallery, Dublin

Sean Scully: Ten Barcelona Paintings, Galerie Bernd Klüser, Munich

1998

Sean Scully: Paintings and Works on Paper, Galerie Bernd Klüser, Munich
Sean Scully: Mirror Images: Paintings & Works on Paper, Timothy Taylor Gallery, London
Sean Scully, Bawag Foundation, Vienna, Austria
Sean Scully, Galerie Haas & Fuchs, Berlin
Sean Scully: Seven Mirrors, Harris and Lewis Stacks, Mira Godard Gallery, Toronto
Sean Scully: New Paintings and Works on Paper, Weinberger Gallery, Copenhagen
Sean Scully, Galeria Antonia Puyo, Zaragoza, Spain
Sean Scully: Pastels, Watercolors, Prints and Photos, Galerie Le Triangle Blue Art Contemporain,
Stavelot, Belgium

1997

Sean Scully: Seven Unions, Timothy Taylor Gallery, London
Sean Scully 1989–1997, La Sala de Exposiciones REKALDE, Bilbao, Spain; traveled to Salas del
Palacio Episcopal, Plaza del Obispo, Málaga, Spain; Fundacio "la Caixa," Palma de Mallorca, Spain
Sean Scully 1982–1996, Manchester City Art Galleries & the Whitworth Art Gallery, Manchester, England
Sean Scully: Recent Paintings, Galerie Lelong, Paris
Sean Scully, Kerlin Gallery, Dublin
Sean Scully: Floating Paintings and Photographs, Galerie Lelong, New York
Sean Scully: Obra Reciente: Pinturas, Acuarelas, Pasteles y Obra Grafica, Galeria DV, San Sebastian, Spain
Sean Scully, Mary Boone Gallery, New York
Sean Scully: Paintings & Works on Paper, Galerie Jamileh Weber, Zürich
Sean Scully: Prints and Watercolors, John Berggruen Gallery, San Francisco

1996

Sean Scully: The Catherine Paintings (1979–1995) & Watercolours, Casino Luxembourg, Forum d'art
contemporain, Luxembourg
Sean Scully: Obra grafica reciente, Edicions T Galeria D'Art, Barcelona
Sean Scully: Paintings and Works on Paper, Galerie nationale du Jeu de Paume, Paris; traveled to
Neue Galerie der Stadt Linz, Linz, Austria; Culturgest, Lisbon, Portugal
Sean Scully, curated by Danilo Eccher, Galleria d'Arte Moderna – Villa Delle Rose, Bologna, Italy
Sean Scully, Galeria Carles Taché, Barcelona
Sean Scully: New Pastels, Galerie Lelong, New York
Sean Scully: Graphische Arbeiten, Galerie Angelika Harthan, Stuttgart, Germany
Sean Scully: Works on Paper 1975–1996, Staatliche Graphische Sammlung, Neue Pinakothek, Munich;
traveled to Museum Folkwang Essen, Essen, Germany; Henie-Onstad Kunstsenter, Hovikodden,
Norway; Whitworth Art Gallery, Manchester, England; Dublin City Gallery The Hugh Lane, Dublin;
as *Sean Scully: Works on Paper 1984–1996*, Herning Kunstmuseum, Herning, Denmark; Milwaukee
Art Museum, Milwaukee, Wisconsin; Denver Art Museum, Denver, Colorado; Carpenter Center
for the Visual Arts, Harvard University, Cambridge, Massachusetts; Albright-Knox Art Gallery,
Buffalo, New York

1995

Sean Scully, Galeria De L'Ancien College, Châtellerault, France
Sean Scully, Waddington Galleries, London
Sean Scully: The Beauty of the Real, Galerie Bernd Klüser, Munich
Sean Scully: Twenty Years 1976–1995, Hirshhorn Museum and Sculpture Garden, Smithsonian
Institution, Washington, D.C.; traveled to the High Museum of Art, Atlanta, Georgia; Fundacio
"la Caixa" Centre Cultural, Barcelona; Irish Museum of Modern Art, Dublin; Schirn Kunsthalle
Frankfurt, Frankfurt am Main, Germany
Sean Scully: The Catherine Paintings, Kunsthalle Bielefeld, Bielefeld, Germany; traveled to Palais des
Beaux-Arts, Charleroi, Belgium
Sean Scully, Mary Boone Gallery, New York

1994

Sean Scully: The Light in the Darkness, Fuji Television Gallery, Tokyo
Sean Scully: Works on Paper, Knoedler & Co., New York
Sean Scully: Paintings, Butler Gallery, Kilkenny Castle, Kilkenny, Ireland
Sean Scully, Kerlin Gallery, Dublin
Sean Scully: Obra graphica 1991–1994, Galeria DV, San Sebastian, Spain
Sean Scully: La Forma e lo Spirito / Sean Scully: The Form and the Spirit, Galleria Gian Ferrari Arte
Contemporanea, Milan, Italy

1993

Sean Scully, Mary Boone Gallery, New York
Sean Scully: The Catherine Paintings, Modern Art Museum of Fort Worth, Fort Worth, Texas
Sean Scully: Heart of Darkness, Waddington Galleries, London
Sean Scully: Paintings and Works on Paper, Galerie Bernd Klüser, Munich

1992

Sean Scully: New Graphic Works, Weinberger Gallery, Copenhagen
Sean Scully: Woodcuts, Pamela Auchincloss Gallery, New York
Sean Scully: Prints and Related Works, Brooke Alexander Editions, New York
Sean Scully: New Prints, Bobbie Greenfield Fine Art, Inc., Venice, California
Sean Scully: Woodcuts, Stephen Solovy Fine Art, Chicago
Sean Scully, Daniel Weinberg Gallery, Santa Monica, California
Sean Scully: Paintings 1973–1992, Sert Gallery, Carpenter Center for the Visual Arts, Harvard
University, Cambridge, Massachusetts
Sean Scully, Waddington Galleries, London

1991

Sean Scully: Paintings and Works on Paper, Galerie Jamileh Weber, Zürich

1990

Sean Scully: Prints, M. Art, Tokyo

Sean Scully, Galerie de France, Paris
Sean Scully: Monotypes from the Garner Tullis Workshop, Pamela Auchincloss Gallery, New York
Sean Scully: New Paintings, McKee Gallery, New York

1989
Sean Scully: New Paintings, McKee Gallery, New York
Sean Scully: Paintings and Works on Paper 1982–1988, Whitechapel Art Gallery, London; traveled to Centro de Arte Reina Sofia – Palacio de Velázquez, Parque del Retiro, Madrid; Städtische Galerie im Lenbachhaus, Munich
Sean Scully: Pastel Drawings, Grob Gallery, London
Sean Scully: Bilder und Zeichnungen, Galerie Karsten Greve, Cologne, Germany

1988
Sean Scully, Fuji Television Gallery, Tokyo

1987
Sean Scully: Monotypes from the Garner Tullis Workshop, Pamela Auchincloss Gallery, Santa Barbara, California
Sean Scully: Monotypes, McKee Gallery, New York
Sean Scully: Recent Monotypes and Drawings, Flanders Contemporary Art, Minneapolis, Minnesota
Sean Scully, Mayor Rowan Gallery, London
Sean Scully, Galerie Schmela, Düsseldorf, Germany
Sean Scully: Matrix / Berkeley 112, University Art Museum, University of California at Berkeley, Berkeley, California
Sean Scully, curated by Neal Benezra, Art Institute of Chicago, Chicago

1986
Sean Scully: Paintings 1985–1986, McKee Gallery, New York

1985
Sean Scully: New Paintings, McKee Gallery, New York
Sean Scully: Paintings and Drawings, Barbara Krakow Gallery, Boston, Massachusetts
Sean Scully, Museum of Art, Carnegie Institute, Pittsburg, Pennsylvania; traveled to Museum of Fine Arts, Boston, Massachusetts
Sean Scully: Neue Arbeiten, Galerie Schmela, Düsseldorf, Germany

1984
Sean Scully: Recent Paintings and Drawings, Juda Rowan Gallery, London
Sean Scully: schilderijen – tekeningen, Galerij S65, Aalst, Belgium

1983
Sean Scully, McKee Gallery, New York

1982
Sean Scully: Recent Paintings, William Beadleston Inc., New York

1981
Sean Scully, Susan Caldwell Inc., New York
Sean Scully: Recent Paintings, Rowan Gallery, London
Sean Scully: Seven Drawings, a Wall Painting: Spider* *to the people of Berlin – dedicated to Blinky Palermo, Museum für (Sub-) Kultur, Berlin
Sean Scully: Paintings 1971–1981, Ikon Gallery, Birmingham, England; traveled under the auspices of the Arts Council of Great Britain to Ceolfrith Gallery, Sunderland Arts Centre, Sunderland, England; Douglas Hyde Gallery, Dublin; Warwick Arts Trust, London
Sean Scully: Recent Paintings, McIntosh/Drysdale Gallery, Washington, D.C.

1980
Sean Scully, Susan Caldwell Inc., New York

1979
Painting for One Place, Peter Nadin's Space, New York
Sean Scully: Recent Paintings, Rowan Gallery, London
Sean Scully: Paintings 1975–1979, The Clocktower, New York

1977
Sean Scully, Duffy / Gibbs Gallery, New York
Sean Scully: Paintings & Drawings, Rowan Gallery, London

1976
Sean Scully: Works on Paper, La Tortue Gallery, Santa Monica, California

1975
Sean Scully: Paintings 1974, La Tortue Gallery, Santa Monica, California
Sean Scully: Recent Paintings, Rowan Gallery, London

1973
Sean Scully: Recent Paintings, Rowan Gallery, London

1972
Sean Scully, Bookshop Gallery, Ceolfrith Art Centre, Sunderland, England

GROUP EXHIBITIONS

2017
The Horizontal, Cheim & Read, New York
Park, Guangzhou, Holly's Gallery, Guangzhou, China
Park, Hong Kong, G/F (LIGHTSTAGE), Hong Kong
The Power of the Avant-garde, National Museum, Krakow, The Feliks Jasienski Szolayski House
Against Landscape, Coniston Institute & Ruskin Museum, Cumbria, England; traveled to Glasgow
School of Art, Scotland
Sean Scully – Liliane Tomasko, Centre d'art Contemporain Acentmetresdumonde, Perpignan, France
Peter and Alison Klein Collection, Kunstwerk – Sammlung Alison and Peter W. Klein, Eberdingen-
Nussdorf, Germany
Selected Works from the Hubert Looser Collection, National Gallery at the National Museum of
Norway, Olso, Norway
Abstract Painting Now!, Kunsthalle Krems, Krems, Austria
Über den Umgang mit Menschen, wenn Zuneigung im Spiel ist. Sammlung Klein, Kunstmuseum
Stuttgart, Stuttgart, Germany

2016
As If, At Home, curated by Jurriaan Benschop, Berlin-Friedrichshain, BOX Freiraum, Germany
Chers Amis, Musée National d'Art Moderne, Centre Georges Pompidou, Paris
Summer Exhibition 2016, Royal Academy of Arts, London
Jacob Kainen, Thomas Nozkowski, and Sean Scully, Hemphill Fine Arts, Washington, D.C.
Testing Testing: Painting and Sculpture since 1960 from the Permanent Collection, Ackland Art
Museum, University of North Carolina at Chapel Hill, North Carolina
The Power of the Avant-garde, Centre for Fine Arts, Palais des Beaux-Arts, Paleis voor Schone
Kunsten, Brussels, Belgium
DIALOGUES, The Looser Collection. Museum Folkwang, Essen, Germany
BASQUIAT, DUBUFFET, SOULAGES . . . A Private Collection, Foundation Hermitage, Lausanne, Switzerland
Sean Scully – Liliane Tomasko, Centro Cultural Bancaja, Valencia, Spain
Architecture of Color: The Legacy of Luis Barragán, Timothy Taylor Gallery, New York
Euroscope: La collection de la Banque européenne d'investissement au Cercle Cité, Cercle Cité, Luxembourg
Passion and Commitment: The Art of Luther Brady, Freedman Art, New York
Wir sind was wir sammeln (We Are What We Collect), Museum Lothar Fischer, Neumarkt, Germany
ING Discerning Eye Exhibition, Mall Galleries, London
Resistance and Persistence, Ingleby Gallery, Edinburgh, Scotland
Night in the Museum: Ryan Gander curates the Arts Council Collection, Birmingham Museum & Art
Gallery, Birmingham, England
Kirchner, Léger, Scully & more: Works from the Collection, Hilti Art Foundation, Kunstmuseum
Liechtenstein, Vaduz, Liechtenstein
Just Black and White, Galerie Klüser, Munich
Modernist Intersections: The Tia Collection, University of Arizona Museum of Art, Tucson, Arizona
Group Show of Editions, Nicholas Gallery, Belfast, Ireland

2015

Surface Tension, The FLAG Foundation, New York

Galerie Lelong, Salas Municipales de Exposiciones de la Iglesia de las Francesas y del Museo de la Pasion, Valladolid, Spain

Ein Moment-ewig, Kunstwerk Sammlung Alison und Peter W. Klein, Stuttgart, Germany

The Patton Collection: A Gift to North Carolina, North Carolina Museum of Art, Raleigh, North Carolina

Meet Me Halfway: Selections from the Anita Reiner Collection, Cristin Tierney Gallery, New York

Stoney Road Press Limited Edition Books, Stoney Road Press, Dublin

2014

5 Years Schellingstrabe, Walter Storms Galerie, Munich

Contemporary Art: Selections from the Museum's Collection, Museum of Fine Arts, Houston, Texas

Couleurs Contemporaines, Centre D'Art de Chateauvert, Chateauvert, France

The Phillips Collection: Picasso and Great Artists, Daejeon Museum of Art, Daejeon, Korea; traveled to Seoul Arts Center, Seoul, Korea

Record'Art, Cadaques, Girona, Spain

The Artist's Eye, Hunt Museum, Limerick, Ireland

Summer Exhibition, Royal Academy of Arts, London

Back to the Future: Drawings from Tiepolo to Warhol, The Klüser Collection, Kunsthalle Krems, Krems, Austria

Post-Picasso: Reaccions Contemporaneas (Post-Picasso: Contemporary Reactions), Museu Picasso, Barcelona

B/W, Timothy Taylor Gallery, London

Encounter: Royal Academy of Arts in China, Yuan Museum, Beijing

2013

Summer Exhibition, Royal Academy of Arts, London

Marokkanische Teppiche und Die Kunst Der Moderne. Moroccan Carpets and Modern Art, Florian Hufnagl, Die Heue Sammlung, International Design Museum, Munich

Farbiges Grau, Mies van der Rohe Haus, Berlin

Edge, Order, Rupture, Galerie Lelong, New York

Entre Bambalinas . . . Arte y Moda, Institut Valencià d'Art Modern (IVAM), Valencia, Spain

93, Centro Galego de Arte Contemporanea, A Coruña, Spain

2012

Window to the World: From Dürer to Mondrian and Beyond, Looking Through the Window of Art from the Renaissance to Today, Museo Cantonale d'Arte e Museo d'Arte, Lugano, Switzerland; traveled to Fondation de l'Hermitage, Lausanne, Switzerland

Abstract Drawings, Smithsonian American Art Museum, Washington, D.C.

Stimuli: Prints and Multiples, Alexander and Bonin, New York

Bremerhaven-Berlin-Aichach: 35 artworks from 3 places and 37 years, Zweigstelle Berlin, Berlin

"Chemin faisant . . .”, Musee jurassien des Arts, Moutier, Switzerland

Summer Exhibition, Royal Academy of Arts, London

2011

Selected Prints, Galerie Klüser, Munich

Photography: Richard Deacon, Frederick Hammersley, Sean Scully, Juan Uslé, L.A. Louver, Venice, California

Group Exhibition, Firestone Library, Rare Books & Special Collections, Princeton University, Princeton, New Jersey

The Shadow of the Corner of the Wall. Liliane Tomasko and Sean Scully, Das Haus am Lützowplatz, Berlin

Zettels Traum: Die Zeichnungssammlung Bern und Verena Klüser, Von Der Heydt – Museum, Wuppertal, Germany

The Cincinnati Art Award: Gifts and Warhol Portraits of Doug Cramer, Cincinnati Art Museum, Cincinnati, Ohio

Eroi / Heroes, Galleria Civica D'Arte Moderna e Contemporanea, Torino, Italy

The Minimal Gesture, Timothy Taylor Gallery, London

Gravity, Crawford Art Gallery, Cork, Ireland

Planos Sensibles, Museo de Arte Contemporáneo, Alicante, Spain

Body and Soul: Lawrence Carroll, Gotthard Graubner, Sean Scully, Hôtel des Arts, Toulon, France

The Indiscipline of Painting: International abstraction from the 1960s to now, Tate St. Ives, St. Ives, Cornwall, England; traveled to Mead Gallery, Warwick Arts Centre, Coventry, England

Multiplicity, Smithsonian American Art Museum, Washington, D.C.

2010

Kunstwerke aus der UBS Art Collection im Opern Turm Frankfurt, Der Opern Turm, Frankfurt, Germany

From Homer to Hopper: American Watercolor Masterworks from the Currier Museum of Art, Currier Museum of Art, Manchester, New Hampshire

More Photographs Than Bricks, Luther W. Brady Art Gallery, George Washington University, Washington, D.C.

Living With Art: Collecting Contemporary in Metro New York, Neuberger Museum of Art, Purchase, New York

Summer Exhibition 2010, Royal Academy of Arts, London

Calder to Warhol: Introducing the Fisher Collection, San Francisco Museum of Modern Art, San Francisco

The Hugh Lane Centenary Print Collection, Linehall Arts Centre, Castlebar, Ireland

Decameron, curated by David Cohen, New York Studio School, New York

The Moderns: The Arts in Ireland from the 1900s to the 1970s, Irish Museum of Modern Art, Dublin

17 Malern, Bayerische Akademie der Schönon Künste, Munich

2009

Building with Colour, curated by Helen Baker, Gallery North, Northumbria University, Newcastle upon Tyne, England

Drei. Das Triptychon in der Moderne, Kunstmuseum Stuttgart, Stuttgart, Germany

Regards Croises: Les oeuvres de la BEI à la BCEE, Galerie d'art contemporain Am Tunnel & Espace Edward Steichen, Luxembourg

Second Biennial of the Canary Islands, CAAM – Los Balcones 11 y 13, Las Palmas De Gran Canaria, Spain

Pop to Present, Pigott Family Gallery, Iris & B. Gerald Cantor Center for Visual Arts, Stanford University, Stanford, California

Shaping Reality: Geometric Abstraction after 1960, Minneapolis Institute of Arts, Minneapolis, Minnesota
Passports, curated by Michael Craig-Martin and Andrea Rose, Whitechapel Gallery, London; and Padiglione d'Arte Contemporanea, Milan, Italy
1999 / 2009, Regard Sur La Collection Du Conseil Général Du Var, Hôtel des Arts, Toulon, France
Markierungen, Sean Scully & Jannis Kounellis, 401 Contemporary, Berlin
Historias del Confín, Institut Valencià d'Art Modern (IVAM), Valencia, Spain
IN-FINITUM, 53rd Venice Biennale, Palazzo Fortuny, Venice, Italy
The Weight of Light, curated by Carissa Farrell, VISUAL Centre for Contemporary Art, Carlow, Ireland

2008
Masterpieces of Modern British Art: Selected Works from the Derek Williams Trust and Amgueddfa Cymru National Museum Wales, Osborne Samuel Gallery, London
Art Is for the Spirit: Works from the UBS Art Collection, Mori Art Museum, Tokyo
MAXImin, Maximum Minimization in Contemporary Art, Fundación Juan March, Madrid
Degas to Diebenkorn: The Phillips Collects, Phillips Collection, Washington, D.C.
Monet-Kandinsky-Rothko und die folgen Wege der abstrakten Malerei, BA-CA Kunstforum Wien, Palais Ferstel, Vienna, Austria
Unique Act: Five Abstract Painters, curated by Barbara Dawson, Dublin City Gallery The Hugh Lane, Dublin
New Horizons: The Collection of the Ishibashi Foundation, Bridgestone Museum of Art, Ishibashi Foundation, Tokyo
Rhythmus 21 – Positionen des Abstrakten, Städtische Galerie im Lenbachhaus, Munich
Paper Trail II: Passing Through Clouds, Rose Art Museum, Brandeis University, Waltham, Massachusetts
The 183rd Annual: An Invitational Exhibition of Contemporary American Art, National Academy Museum & School of Fine Arts, New York
A Year in Drawing, Galerie Lelong, New York
Reflections on Light: 30 Years Galerie Bernd Klüser, Galerie Bernd Klüser, Munich
Camouflage II, curated by Helmut Friedel and Giovanni Iovane, Galleria Gentili, Prato, Italy
Hugh Lane Centenary Print Collection, Dublin City Gallery The Hugh Lane, Dublin
Made in Munich, Haus der Kunst, Munich
Fifty Percent Solitude, Kerlin Gallery, Dublin
Color into Light, Museum of Fine Arts, Houston, Texas

2007
Klasse Scully, whiteBOX e.v., Kultfabrik, Munich
Radharc, Galway Arts Centre, Galway, Ireland
Beckett, Centre Georges Pompidou, Paris
(I'm Always Touched) By Your Presence, Dear: New Acquisitions, Irish Museum of Modern Art, Dublin
Before and After Minimalism: A Century of Abstract Tendencies in the Daimler Chrysler Collection, Museu d'Art Espanyol Contemporani Fundación Juan March, Palma de Mallorca, Spain
Große Malerei, Lentos Kunstmuseum Linz, Linz, Austria
Collecting the Past, Present, Future – Highlights of British Art from Turner to Freud, Abbot Hall Art

Gallery, Kendal, England
Themes and Variations in Painting and Sculpture, Museum of Fine Arts, Houston, Texas
Frisch Gestrichen, Museum Franz Gertsch, Burgdorf, Switzerland
DE-Natured. Painting, Sculpture and Work on Paper from the Anderson Collection + the Anderson Graphic Arts Collection, curated by Heather Pamela Green, San Jose Museum of Art, San Jose, California
No answer is also an answer – Recent acquisitions 2005–2007, Irish Museum of Modern Art, Dublin
La vida privada – Coleccion Josep Civit, Centro de Arte y Naturaleza – Fundación Beulas, Huesca, Spain
Freshly Painted: Worlds from the Willy Michel Collection, Museum Franz Gertsch, Burgdorf, Switzerland
Group Show – Painting II, McKee Gallery, New York

2006
Big Juicy Paintings (and more): Selections from the Permanent Collection, curated by Peter Boswell, Miami Art Museum, Miami, Florida
Nomaden im Kunstsalon – Begegnungen mit der Moderne von Bayer bis Sol LeWitt, Lentos Kunstmuseum Linz, Linz, Austria
Homage to Chilida, curated by Kosme de Barañano, Guggenheim Museum Bilbao, Bilbao, Spain
The Unknown Masterpiece, ARTIUM Centro – Museo Vasco de Arte Contemporaneo, Vitoria-Gasteiz, Spain
Kunst und Photographie, Photographie und Kunst, Galerie Bernd Klüser, Munich
Against the Grain: Contemporary Art from the Edward R. Broida Collection, Museum of Modern Art, New York
The Collector's Collection, Ormeau Baths Gallery, Belfast, Northern Ireland
Sammlung Essl – Kunst der Gegenwart, Kunstverein Villa Wessel, Iserlohn, Germany

2005
Von Paul Gauguin bis Imi Knoebel, Werke aus der Hilti art foundation, Kunstmuseum Liechtenstein, Vaduz, Liechtenstein
Western Biennale of Art: Art Tomorrow, curated by Edward Lucie-Smith, John Natsoulas Center for the Arts, Davis, California
After the Thaw – Recent Irish Art from the AIB Collection, Crawford Municipal Art Gallery, Cork, Ireland
The Giving Person, curated by Lorand Hegyi, Fondazione Culturale Edison, Palazzo delle Arti di Napoli, Naples, Italy
Eye of the Storm: The IMMA Collection, Irish Museum of Modern Art, Dublin
Summer Group Show, McKee Gallery, New York
Fotografia, Galeria Estiarte, Madrid, Spain
Minimalism and After IV, DaimlerChrysler Contemporary, Berlin
Points of View: Landscapes and Photography, Galerie Lelong, New York
Summer Group Show, Kerlin Gallery, Dublin
Sean Scully, Stephan Girard, Nicolas Ruel, Galerie Orange Art Contemporain, Montreal, Canada; traveled to Galerie Lacerte Art Contemporain, Quebec City, Canada
Soltanto Un Quadro Al Massimo, Accademia Tedesca Roma Villa Massimo, Rome
Pairings II: Discovered Dialogues in Postwar Abstraction, Hackett-Freedman Gallery, San Francisco
SIAR 50: 50 Years of Irish Art from the Collections of the Contemporary Irish Art Society, curated by Campbell Bruce and Catherine Marshall, Irish Museum of Modern Art, Dublin

2004

Masterprints, Sundsvalls Museum, Sundsvall, Sweden
Picasso to Thiebaud, Cantor Center for Visual Arts, Stanford University, Stanford, California
A Vision of Modern Art, In Memory of Dorothy Walker, Irish Museum of Modern Art, Dublin
Pop Art to Minimalism: The Serial Attitude, Albertina, Vienna, Austria
High Falutin Stuff, Irish Museum of Modern Art, Dublin
Bearings: Landscapes from the IMMA Collection, curated by Marguerite O'Molloy, Irish Museum of
Modern Art, Dublin
In the Time of Shaking. Irish Artists for Amnesty International, Irish Museum of Modern Art, Dublin
Behind Closed Doors, curated by Susan H. Edwards, Katonah Museum of Art, Katonah, New York
Views from an Island and Representing the Tain, Millennium Monument Museum, Beijing; traveled to
Shanghai Art Museum, Shanghai
Monocromos: De Malevich al Presente, curated by Barbara Rose, Museo Nacional Centro de Arte
Reina Sofia, Madrid
Matisse to Freud: A Critic's Choice – The Alexander Walker Bequest, British Museum, London
Bloomsday 16 Juni 1904–16 Juni 2004, Galerie Bernd Klüser, Munich
The Gallery Selects . . . , Alexander and Bonin, New York
Sean Scully / Jon Groom, Galerie 422, Gmunden, Austria
Nueva tecnologia-nueva iconografia-nueva fotografia, Museu d'Arte Español Contemporani, Palma
de Mallorca, Spain; traveled to Museo de Arte Abstracto Español, Cuenca, Spain
Destination Germany, Kunst Galerie Fürth, Fürth, Germany
La Collection, Hôtel des Arts, Toulon, France
Beneath the Sky, Cavan County Museum, Ballyjamesduff, Ireland
Iranische Flachgewebe im Spiegel der Moderne, curated by Isabella Studer-Geisser, Historisches und
Völkerkundemuseum, St. Gallen, Switzerland

2003

Taché a Pelaires (Carroll, Cragg, Kounellis, Rousse, Scully), Centro Cultural Contemporani Pelaires,
Palma de Mallorca, Spain
Abstraction in Photography, Von Lintel Gallery, New York
Human Stories – Photographs and Paintings from the Essl Collection, Ludwig Museum-Museum of
Contemporary Art, Budapest, Hungary
Inaugural Group Show, Timothy Taylor Gallery, London
Avant-garde und Tradition, Lentos Kunstmuseum Linz, Linz, Austria
The Museum Store Collects, Arizona State University Art Museum, Nelson Fine Arts Center,
Tempe, Arizona
Divergent, Galerie Lelong, New York
Streifzüge, Galerie Lelong, Zürich
Nachbarschaften – Arbeiten auf Papier, Galerie Dittmar, Berlin
Drawing Modern: Works from the Agnes Gund Collection, Cleveland Art Institute, Cleveland, Ohio
The Eighties – Part II: USA, Galerie Bernd Klüser, Munich
Grafiikkaa ja piirustuksia, Forum Box, Helsinki, Finland

2002

Selected Works – A Collection, Galerie Jamileh Weber, Zürich

Profile of a Collection: The Gordon Lambert Trust Collection at IMMA, Irish Museum of Modern Art, Dublin

The Rowan Collection: Contemporary British and Irish Art, Irish Museum of Modern Art, Dublin

Augenblick, Foto / Kunst, Sammlung Essl, Klosterneuburg, Vienna, Austria

Choose your partner – An International Drawing Show, Nusser & Baumgart Contemporary, Munich

Abstraction, Ingleby Gallery, Edinburgh, Scotland

25 Bienal De São Paulo, Fundação Bienal De São Paulo, São Paulo, Brazil

Epic Paintings from the Luther W. Brady Collection, Luther W. Brady Art Gallery, George Washington University, Washington, D.C.

Eight New Paintings, Kerlin Gallery, Dublin

Extranjeros – Los Otros Artistas Españoles, Museo de Arte Contemporaneo Esteban Vicente, Segovia, Spain

Margins of Abstraction, curated by Robert Knafo, Kouros Gallery, New York

177th Annual Exhibition, National Academy of Design, New York

No Object, No Subject, No Matter…Abstraction in the IMMA Collection, Irish Museum of Modern Art, Dublin

Independent Visions, John Berggruen Gallery, San Francisco

Watercolor, curated by David Cohen, New York Studio School, New York

Colour & Concept: International Colour Photography, National Gallery of Australia, Canberra, Australia

110 Years: The Permanent Collection of the Modern Art Museum of Fort Worth, Modern Art Museum of Fort Worth, Texas

2001

Group Show, McKee Gallery, New York

Content Is a Glimpse, Timothy Taylor Gallery, London

A Century of Drawing: Works on Paper from Degas to LeWitt, National Gallery of Art, Washington, D.C.

Watercolor: In the Abstract, curated by Pamela Auchincloss; traveled to the Hyde Collection Art Museum, Glen Falls, New York; Michael C. Rockefeller Arts Center Gallery, SUNY College at Fredonia, New York; Butler Institute of American Art, Youngstown, Ohio; Ben Shahn Gallery, William Patterson University, Wayne, New Jersey; Sarah Moody Gallery of Art, University of Alabama, Tuscaloosa, Alabama

2000

Works on Paper, Timothy Taylor Gallery, London

Sean Scully / Eduardo Chillida, Alan Cristea Gallery, London

On Canvas: Contemporary Painting from the Collection, curated by J. Fiona Ragheb, Solomon R. Guggenheim Museum, New York

Art Moves to Benefit the Cure, Benefiting the Christopher Reeve Paralysis Foundation, Bergdorf Goodman, New York; Auction at Sotheby's New York

L'Ombra Della Ragione: L'Idea Del Sacro Nell'Identita Europa Nel XX Secolo, Galleria D'Arte Moderna Bologna, Bologna, Italy

Von Albers bis Paik: Konstruktive Werke aus der Sammlung DaimlerChrylser, Haus für Konstruktive und Konkrete Kunst, Zürich

Colleccion MMKSLW: Viena, de Warhol a Cabrita Reis, Centro Galego de Arte Contemporanea, Santiago de Compostela, Spain

September Selections, Knoedler & Company, New York

Group Show, Timothy Taylor Gallery, London

Une Ville – Une Collection, Centre de la Gravure et de l'Image Imprimee, La Louviere, Belgium

New Works, Galerie Jamileh Weber, Zürich

Import, curated by Catherine Marshall and Marguerite O'Molloy, Irish Museum of Modern Art, Dublin

Shifting Ground. Selected Works of Irish Art 1950–2000, Irish Museum of Modern Art, Dublin

1999

Signature Pieces: Contemporary British Prints and Multiples, Alan Cristea Gallery, London

Unlocking the Grid. Concerning the Grid in Recent Painting, Main Gallery, University of Rhode Island, Kingston, Rhode Island

Side by Side, Knoedler & Company, New York

Geometrie als Gestalt: Strukturen der Modernen Kunst von Albers bis Paik: Werke der Sammlung DaimlerChrysler, Neue Nationalgalerie, Staatliche Museen zu Berlin, Berlin; traveled as *Von Albers bis Paik: Konstuktive Werke aus der Sammlung DaimlerChrysler*, Haus für Konstruktive und Konkrete Kunst, Zürich

The Art of Collecting, Flanders Contemporary Art, Minneapolis, Minnesota

A Land of Heart's Desire – 300 Years of Irish Art, Ulster Museum of Art, Belfast, Northern Ireland

Drawing in the Present Tense, curated by Roger Shephard and George Negroponte, Parsons School of Design, New York; traveled to Eastern Connecticut State University, Willimantic, Connecticut; North Dakota Museum of Art, Grand Forks, North Dakota

Tore A. Holm's Collection of Contemporary European Art – An Encounter between North and South, Centro Cultural del Conde Duque, Madrid

The Essl Collection: The First View, curated by Rudi Fuchs, Sammlung Essl, Klosterneuburg, Vienna, Austria

25 Jahre / 25th Anniversary, Galerie Jamileh Weber, Zürich

Pars Pro Toto, Galerie Lelong, Zürich

1999 Drawings, Alexander + Bonin, New York

Zeitschnitt 1900–2000:100 Jahre, 100 Werke, Lentos Kunstmuseum Linz, Linz, Austria

1998

Zeit und Materie, Baukunst, Cologne, Germany

The Edward R. Broida Collection: A Selection of Works, Orlando Museum of Art, Orlando, Florida

Arterias: Collection of Contemporary Art Fundacio la Caixa, Malmö Konsthal, Malmö, Sweden

45th Corcoran Biennial, Corcoran Gallery of Art, Washington, D.C.

Welcome Back!, Denver Art Museum, Denver, Colorado

Sarajevo 2000, curated by Lorand Heygi, Museum Moderner Kunst Stiftung Ludwig Wein, Palais Liechtenstein, Vienna, Austria

Lawrence Carroll and Sean Scully, Lawing Gallery, Houston, Texas

Cleveland Collects Contemporary Art, Cleveland Museum of Art, Cleveland, Ohio

Contemporary Art: The Janet Wolfson de Botton Gift, Tate Gallery, London
Photographies, Galerie Lelong, Paris
On a Clear Day, Graphische Sammlung, Staatsgalerie Stuttgart, Stuttgart, Germany
Large Scale Works on Paper: Le Va, LeWitt, Mangold, Scully, Serra, Winters, Danese, New York
Jan Dibbets / Sean Scully Fotografias, Galeria Estiarte, Madrid
Group Exhibition, Kerlin Gallery, Dublin
Acquisitions 1997, Le Conseil General du Val-de-Marne FDAC exhibited at Hôtel du Departement, Creteil, France
Matrix Berkeley 1978–1998, University of California, Berkeley Art Museum and Pacific Film Archive, Berkeley, California
En Norsk Samling Au Europeisk Kunst, Trondheim Kunstmuseum, Trondheim, Norway

1997
Without trembling, Galerie Fortlaan 17, Gent, Belgium
After the Fall: Aspects of Abstract Painting Since 1970, curated by Lilly Wei, Newhouse Center for Contemporary Art, Snug Harbor Cultural Center, Staten Island, New York
British Arts Council Collection, Royal Festival Hall, London
The Pursuit of Painting, curated by Stephen McKenna, Irish Museum of Modern Art, Dublin
Prints, Galerie Lelong, New York
Prints, Galerie Lelong, Paris
A Century of Irish Paintings: Selections from the Collection of the Hugh Lane Municipal Gallery of Modern Art, Dublin, Dublin City Gallery The Hugh Lane, Dublin; traveled to Hokkaido Museum of Modern Art, Sapporo, Japan; Mitaka City Gallery of Art, Mitaka, Tokyo; Yamanashi Prefectural Museum of Art, Yamanashi, Japan
The View From Denver: Contemporary American Art from the Denver Art Museum, Museum Moderner Kunst Stiftung Ludwig Wein, Vienna, Austria
Thirty-Five Years at Crown Point Press: Making Prints, Doing Art, National Gallery of Art, Washington, D.C.; traveled to the Fine Arts Museum of San Francisco, San Francisco
Singular Impressions: The Monotype in America, National Museum of American Art, Washington, D.C.

1996
XV Salon des los 16, Museo de Antropologia, Madrid
Balancing Act, Room Gallery, New York
Nuevas Abstracciones, Museo Nacional Centro de Arte Reina Sofia, Madrid; traveled to Kunsthalle Bielefeld, Bielefeld, Germany; Museu d'Art Contemporani de Barcelona, Barcelona
Bare Bones, TZ Art, New York
Festival de Culture Irlandaise Contemporaine, Ecoles des Beaux-Arts, Paris
Thinking Print: Books to Billboards 1980–95, Museum of Modern Art, New York
Holländisches Bad: Radierungen zur Renaissance einer Technik, Kunsthaus, Hamburg, Germany; traveled to Brecht-Haus-Weissensee, Berlin

1995

Seven from the Seventies, Knoedler & Company, New York
New Publications, Brooke Alexander Editions, New York
New York Abstract, curated by Lew Thomas, Contemporary Arts Center, New Orleans, Louisiana
US Prints, Retretti Art Center, Punkaharju, Finland
Color + Structure: Mangold, De Maria, Scully, Swanger, Thursz, Tusek, Tuttle, Galerie Lelong, New York

1994

Paper Under Pressure: Work in Collaboration with Garner Tullis, Sun Valley Center Gallery, Ketchum, Idaho
Recent Painting Acquisitions, Tate Gallery, London
Contemporary Watercolors: Europe and America, curated by Diana Block, University of North Texas Art Gallery, Denton, Texas
For 25 Years: Brooke Alexander Editions, Museum of Modern Art, New York
Recent Acquisitions: Paintings from the Collection, IMMA, Irish Museum of Modern Art, Dublin
An American Passion: The Susan Kasen Summer and Robert D. Summer Collection of Contemporary British Painting, curated by Susie Allen and Stefan van Raay, McLellan Galleries, Glasgow, Scotland; traveled to Royal College of Art, London
L'Incanto e la Trascendenza, Galleria Civica de Arte Contemporanea, Trento, Italy
British Abstract Art. Part I: Painting, Flowers East, London

1993

Tutte le Strade Portano A Roma, Palazzo delle Esposizioni, Rome
Beyond Paint, curated by Maurice Poirier, Tibor de Nagy Gallery, New York
Drawing in Black and White: Contemporary Works from the Collection, Museum of Modern Art, Grolier Club, New York
American and European Prints, Machida City Museum of Arts, Tokyo
American and European Works on Paper, Gallery Martin Wieland, Trier, Germany
Italia-America L'astrazione Redefinita, curated by Demetrio Paparoni, Dicastero Cultura, Galleria Nazionale d'Arte Moderna, Repubblica di San Marino, Italy
Partners, Annely Juda Fine Art, London
25 Years: A Retrospective, Cleveland Center for Contemporary Art, Cleveland, Ohio
New Moderns, Baumgartner Galleries Inc., Washington, D.C.
5 One Person Shows, Galerie Jamileh Weber, Zürich
The Turner Prize 1993, Tate Gallery, London
Ausgewählte Druckgraphik, Galerie Bernd Klüser, Munich

1992

Surface to Surface, Barbara Krakow Gallery, Boston, Massachusetts
Four Series of Prints: Donald Judd, Brice Marden, Sean Scully, Terry Winters, John Berggruen Gallery, San Francisco
Recent Abstract Painting: Ross Bleckner, Kenneth Dingwall, Susan Laufer, Ken Nevadomi, Sean Scully, curated by David S. Rubin, Cleveland Center for Contemporary Art, Cleveland, Ohio
Collaborations in Monotype from the Garner Tullis Workshop, Sert Gallery, Carpenter Center for the

Visual Arts, Harvard University, Cambridge, Massachusetts
Geteilte Bilder: Das Diptychon in der neuen Kunst, Museum Folkwang Essen, Essen, Germany
Behind Bars, curated by Meg O'Rourke, Thread Waxing Space, New York
Color Block Prints of the 20th Century, Associated American Artists, New York
Whitechapel Open, Whitechapel Art Gallery, London
Painted on Press: Recent Abstract Prints, Madison Art Center, Madison, Wisconsin
Monotypes, Woodcuts, Drawings, Europaische Akademie Fur Bildende Kunst, Trier, Germany
Garner Tullis Monotype Survey, SOMA Gallery, San Diego, California
44th Annual Academy-Institute Purchase Exhibition, American Academy of Arts and Letters, New York
Verso Bisanzio, con disincanto, curated by Elio Cappuccio, Galeria Sergio Tossi, Arte
Contemporanea, Prato, Italy

1991
Small Format Works on Paper, John Berggruen Gallery, San Francisco
Postmodern Prints, Victoria and Albert Museum, London
Moses, Richter, Scully, Louver Gallery, New York
La Metafisica Della Luce, curated by Demetrio Paparoni, John Goode Gallery, New York
Large Scale Works on Paper, John Berggruen Gallery, San Francisco

1990
Stripes, Barbara Krakow Gallery, Boston, Massachusetts
Drawing: Joseph Beuys, Paul Rotterdam, Sean Scully, Arnold Herstand & Company, New York
Sean Scully / Donald Sultan: Abstraction / Representation, curated by Michelle Meyers, Stanford
University Art Gallery, Stanford, California
Geometric Abstraction, Marc Richards Gallery, Santa Monica, California
Artists in the Abstract, Weatherspoon Art Gallery, University of North Carolina at Greensboro,
Greensboro, North Carolina

1989
The Elusive Surface: Painting in Three Dimensions, Albuquerque Museum, Albuquerque, New Mexico
Drawing and Related Prints, Castelli Graphics, New York
Essential Painting: Kelly, LeWitt, Mangold, Scully, curated by Deborah Leveton, Nelson-Atkins
Museum of Art, Kansas City, Missouri
The 1980s: Prints from the Collection of Joshua P. Smith, National Gallery of Art, Washington, D.C.
The Linear Image: American Masterworks on Paper, curated by Sam Hunter, Marisa del Re Gallery,
New York

1988
17 Years at the Barn, Rosa Esman Gallery, New York
In Side, Barbara Krakow Gallery, Boston, Massachusetts
Works on Paper: Selections from the Garner Tullis Workshop, Pamela Auchincloss Gallery, New York
New Editions, Crown Point Press, San Francisco and New York

Large Works on Paper, Mayor Rowan Gallery, London

Sightings: Drawings with Color, curated by Max Gimblett and Eleanor Moretta, Pratt Manhattan Gallery, Pratt Institute, New York; traveled to Instituto de Estudios Norteamericanos, Barcelona

Sean Scully & Jose Maria Sicilia, New Editions, Crown Point Press, San Francisco, New York

The Presence of Painting: Aspects of British Abstraction 1957–1988, Mappin Art Gallery, Sheffield, England; traveled to Laing Art Gallery, Newcastle upon Tyne, England; Hatton Gallery, Newcastle upon Tyne, England; Ikon Gallery, Birmingham, England; Harris Museum & Art Gallery, Preston, England

1987

The Fortieth Biennial Exhibition of Contemporary American Painting, curated by Ned Rifkin, Corcoran Gallery of Art, Washington, D.C.

Large Scale Prints, Barbara Krakow Gallery, Boston, Massachusetts

Harvey Quaytman and Sean Scully, Ateneum, Helsinki Festival, Helsinki, Finland

Drawing from the 80s – Chatsworth Collaboration, Carnegie Mellon University Art Gallery, Pittsburgh, Pennsylvania

Drawn-Out, Kansas City Art Institute, Kansas City, Missouri

Magic in the Minds Eye: Part 1 & 2, Meadow Brook Art Gallery, Rochester, Michigan

Logical Foundations, curated by the Advisory Services, Museum of Modern Art, New York

Works on Paper, Nina Freundenheim Gallery, Buffalo, New York

Winter, Museum of Modern Art, New York

Large Works by Rowan Artists, Mayor Rowan Gallery, London

Monotypes by Catherine Lee, John Walker, Sean Scully, Rubin Gallery, New York

1986

After Matisse, curated by Tiffany Bell, organized by Independent Curators Inc., New York; traveled to Queens Museum, Flushing, New York; Chrysler Museum, Norfolk, Virginia; Portland Museum of Art, Portland, Maine; Bass Museum of Art, Miami Beach, Florida; Phillips Collection, Washington, D.C.; Dayton Art Institute, Dayton, Ohio; Worcester Art Museum, Worcester, Massachusetts

An American Renaissance in Art: Painting and Sculpture since 1940, Fort Lauderdale Museum of Fine Art, Fort Lauderdale, Florida

Public and Private: American Prints Today, Brooklyn Museum of Art, New York

Catherine Lee & Sean Scully, Cava Gallery, Philadelphia, Pennsylvania

CAL Collects 1, University Art Museum, University of California, Berkeley, Berkeley, California

The Heroic Sublime, Charles Cowles Gallery, New York

Structure / Abstraction, Hill Gallery, Birmingham, Michigan

Courtesy of David McKee, McKee Gallery, New York; traveled to Pamela Auchincloss Gallery, Santa Barbara, California

Detroiters Collect: New Generation, Meadow Brook Art Gallery, Oakland University, Rochester, Michigan

Recent Acquisitions, Contemporary Arts Center, Honolulu, Hawaii

Group Drawing Show, Barbara Krakow Gallery, Boston, Massachusetts

25 Years: Three Decades of Contemporary Art, Judah Rowan Gallery, London

1985

Abstract Painting as Surface and Object, curated by Judith K. Collischan Van Wagner, Hillwood Art Gallery, C.W. Post Center, Long Island University, Brookeville, New York

An Invitational, curated by Tiffany Bell, Condeso / Lawler Gallery, New York

A Decade of Visual Arts at Princeton: Faculty 1975–1985, Princeton University Museum of Art, Princeton, New Jersey

Abstraction / Issues, Tibor de Nagy Gallery, New York; traveled to Oscarsson Hood Gallery, New York; Sherry French Gallery, New York

Art on Paper, Weatherspoon Art Gallery, University of North Carolina at Greensboro, Greensboro, North Carolina

Masterpieces of the Avant-garde, Annely Juda Fine Art / Juda Rowan Gallery, London

Painting 1985, Pam Adler Gallery, New York

Small Work, Juda Rowan Gallery, London

1984

Form Color Surface: Painting About Itself, Barbara Krakow Gallery, Boston, Massachusetts

An International Survey of Recent Painting and Sculpture, Museum of Modern Art, New York

Four Painters: Pat Steir, Sean Scully, Robert Mangold, Robert S. Zakanitch, McIntosh / Drysdale Gallery, Houston, Texas

Part 1: Twelve Abstract Painters, Siegel Contemporary Art, New York

ROSC '84: The Poetry of Vision, Guinness Hop Store, St. James's Gate, Dublin

Currents #6, Milwaukee Art Museum, Milwaukee, Wisconsin

Small Works: New Abstract Painting, Lafayette College and Muhlenberg College, Allentown, Pennsylvania

Group Exhibition, Susan Montezinos Gallery, Philadelphia, Pennsylvania

Hassam & Speicher Purchase Fund Exhibition, Academy of Arts and Letters, New York

Contemporary Paintings and Sculpture, William Beadleston Fine Art Inc., New York

Art on Paper, Galerij S65, Aalst, Belgium

1983

Three Painters: Sean Scully, David Reed, Ted Stamm, Zenith Gallery, Pittsburgh, Pennsylvania

American Abstract Artists, Weatherspoon Art Gallery, University of North Carolina, Greensboro, North Carolina; traveled to Moody Gallery of Art, University of Alabama, Tuscaloosa, Alabama

Nocturne, curated by Michael Walls, Siegel Contemporary Art, New York

New Work New York (Newcastle Salutes New York), Newcastle Polytechnic Art Gallery, Newcastle upon Tyne, England

Student's Choice Exhibition, Yale University Art Gallery, New Haven, Connecticut

Contemporary Abstract Painting, Muhlenberg College Center for the Arts, Allentown, Pennsylvania

1982

Critical Perspectives, curated by Joseph Masheck, P.S.1 The Institute for Art & Urban Resources, New York

Recent Aspects of All-Over, curated by Theodore Bonin, Harm Bouckaert Gallery, New York

Pair Group: Current and Emerging Styles in Abstract Painting, curated by William Zimmer, Jersey City Museum, Jersey City, New Jersey
Workshop F, Chelsea School of Art, London
Group Invitational, Sunne Savage Gallery, Boston, Massachusetts
Art for a New Year, organized by Art Lending Service, Museum of Modern Art, New York

1981
Arabia Felix, curated by William Zimmer, Art Galaxy Gallery, New York
Catherine Porter Scully / Sean Scully: Arbeiten and Wandmalerei, Museum für (Sub-) Kultur, Berlin
New Directions, curated by Sam Hunter, Sidney Janis Gallery, New York
Art for Collectors, Museum of Art, Rhode Island School of Design, Providence, Rhode Island
New Directions: Contemporary American Art from the Commodities Corporation Collection, Museum of Art, Fort Lauderdale, Florida; traveled to the Oklahoma Museum of Art, Oklahoma City, Oklahoma; Santa Barbara Museum of Art, Santa Barbara, California; Grand Rapids Art Museum, Grand Rapids, Michigan; Madison Art Center, Madison, Wisconsin; Montgomery Museum of Fine Arts, Montgomery, Alabama

1980
Marking Black, Bronx Museum of the Arts, New York
New Directions, Princeton University Art Museum, Princeton, New Jersey
The Newcastle Connection, curated by Mary-Helen Wood, Polytechnic Art Gallery, Newcastle upon Tyne, England
The International Connection, Sense of Ireland Festival, Roundhouse Gallery, London
Growing Up with Art, Leicestershire Collection for Schools and Colleges, Whitechapel Art Gallery, London
ROSC, University College Gallery and National Gallery of Ireland, Dublin
Irish Art 1943–1973, Crawford Municipal Art Gallery, Cork, Ireland; traveled to Ulster Museum, Belfast, Ireland

1979
New Wave Painting, curated by Per Jensen, The Clocktower, New York
Fourteen Painters, Lehmann College Art Gallery, City University of New York
First Exhibition, Toni Birkhead Gallery, Cincinnati, Ohio
The British Art Show, curated by William Packer, Mappin Art Gallery, Sheffield, England; traveled to Laing Art Gallery, Newcastle upon Tyne, England; Hatton Art Gallery, Newcastle upon Tyne, England; University Gallery, University of Newcastle, Newcastle upon Tyne, England; Arnolfini, Bristol, England; Bristol and Royal West of England Academy, Bristol, England
Susan Caldwell Gallery, New York
Tolly Cobbold Eastern Arts 2nd National Exhibition, Fitzwilliam Museum, Cambridge, England (traveling exhibition)

1978

Certain Traditions: Recent British and Canadian Art, Edmonton Art Gallery, Edmonton, Canada; traveled to Glenbow-Alberta Institute, Calgary, Canada; Mendel Art Gallery, Saskatoon, Canada; Art Gallery of Windsor, Windsor, Canada; Art Gallery of Hamilton, Hamilton, Canada; London Regional Art Gallery, London; Mostyn Art Gallery, Llandudno, Wales
Rowan Gallery, London
Small Works, Newcastle Polytechnic Art Gallery, Newcastle upon Tyne, England

1977

Post-Minimal Works, curated by Per Jensen, Nobe Gallery, New York
British Painting 1952–1977, Royal Academy of Arts, London
Works on Paper – The Contemporary Art Society's Gifts to Public Galleries 1952–1977, Diploma Galleries, Royal Academy of Arts, London
Rowan Gallery, London

1976

Invitational, John Weber Gallery, New York
7 Artists from the Rowan Gallery, Sunderland Arts Centre, Sunderland, England
Rowan Gallery, London
Invitational Exhibition, Susan Caldwell Gallery, New York

1975

Contemporary Art Society Art Fair, Contemporary Art Society, Mall Galleries, London
The British Art Coming: Contemporary British Art, De Cordova Museum, Lincoln, Massachusetts
Rowan Gallery, London
The Arts Club, London

1974

Dixieme Biennale Internationale D'Art De Menton, Palais De L'Europe, Menton, France
British Painting '74, Hayward Art Gallery, London
John Moores Liverpool Exhibition 9, Walker Art Gallery, Liverpool, England
Rowan Gallery, London

1973

La Peinture Anglaise Aujourd'hui, Musée d'Art Moderne de la Ville de Paris, Paris
Critics Choice, curated by William Varley, Gulbenkian Gallery, People's Theatre, Newcastle upon Tyne, England

1972

John Moores Liverpool Exhibition 8, Walker Art Gallery, Liverpool, England
Northern Young Painters, Stirling University, Stirling, Scotland

1971

Art Spectrum North, Leeds City Art Gallery, Leeds, England; traveled to Laing Art Gallery,

Newcastle upon Tyne, England; Manchester City Art Gallery, Manchester, England
Annual Students' Summer Exhibition, Hatton Gallery, University of Newcastle, Newcastle upon Tyne, England

1970
Northern Young Contemporaries, Whitworth Art Gallery, University of Manchester, Manchester, England
Young Contemporaries, Royal Academy, London; traveled under the auspices of the Arts Council of Great Britain

SITE–SPECIFIC WORK

2016
China Piled Up, commissioned by the London-based Timothy Taylor Gallery, produced following an invitation by the West Bund Art & Design Fair, on display in Shanghai's West Bund area as part of a project called *Xian Chang (On the ground)*, China

2011
Paintings for the lecture hall, KPMG, Frederiksberg, Denmark

2009
Painting for Frederik 8.s Palæ, Amalienborg, Copenhagen, Denmark

2004
Painting, *Et skib er ikke en ø*, for Takkelloftets Foyer, Operaen, Copenhagen, Denmark

AWARDS

2016	Harper's Bazaar Art International Artist of the Year Award, Hong Kong
2015	V Congreso Asociacion Protecturi, Madrid, Spain, for contribution to Spanish religious heritage
2014	Honorary Degree, Doctor of Letters, National University of Ireland, Galway
2013	Becomes member of the Royal Academy of the Arts, London
2010	Honorary Degree, Doctor of Letters, Newcastle University
2008	Honorary Degree, Doctor Honoris Causa, Universitas Miguel Hernandez
2003	Honorary Degree, Doctorate of Fine Arts, Massachusetts College of Art, Boston, and National University of Ireland
2001	Becomes member of Aosdána, Ireland
2000	Honorary Member of the London Institute of Arts and Letters
1984	National Endowment for the Arts Fellowship
1983	National Endowment for the Arts Fellowship
	Guggenheim Fellowship
1972	John Knox Fellowship

PUBLIC COLLECTIONS

Abbott Hall Art Gallery, Kendal, England
Ackland Art Museum, University of North Carolina at Chapel Hill, North Carolina
Akademie der Bildenden Künste, Munich, Germany
Albertina, Vienna, Austria
Albright-Knox Art Gallery, Buffalo, New York
Allied Irish Banks Corporation, Dublin
Anderson Collection at Stanford University, Stanford, California
Arkansas Arts Center Foundation Collection, Little Rock, Arkansas
ARS AEVI Museum of Contemporary Art, Sarajevo, Yugoslavia
Art Gallery of New South Wales, Adelaide, Australia
Art Gallery of New South Wales, Sydney, Australia
Art Gallery of Ontario, Ontario, Canada
Art Gallery of South Australia, Adelaide, South Australia
Art Institute of Chicago, Chicago, Illinois
Arts and Humanities Research Council, Bristol, England
Arts Council of Great Britain, London
AXA Belgique, Brussels, Belgium
Banque Européenne d'Investissement, Luxembourg
BAWAG Foundation, Vienna, Austria
Bibliotheque Nationale de France, Paris
Birmingham Museum of Art, Birmingham, England
Bridgestone Museum of Art, Ishibashi Foundation, Tokyo
British Council Art Collection, London
British Museum, London
Broad Art Foundation, Los Angeles, California
Carnegie Museum of Art, Pittsburgh, Pennsylvania
Carpenter Center for the Visual Arts, Harvard University, Cambridge, Massachusetts
Centre de la gravure et de l'image imprimee, La Louviere, Belgium
Centre National des Artes Plastiques, Paris
Ceolfrith Arts Centre, Sunderland, England
Chase Manhattan Bank, New York
Chatsworth House, Derbyshire, England
Chazen Museum of Art, University of Wisconsin, Madison, Wisconsin
Chemical Bank, New York
Cincinnati Art Museum, Cincinnati, Ohio
Cleveland Museum of Art, Cleveland, Ohio
Coleccion Conei, Barcelona
Consejería de cultura, Santander, Spain
Contemporary Art Society, London
Contemporary Museum, Honolulu, Hawaii

Corcoran Gallery of Art, Washington, D.C.
Council of National Academic Awards, Arts & Humanities Research Council Art Collection,
Bristol, England
Crawford Municipal Art Gallery, Cork, Ireland
Daimler Art Collection, Stuttgart, Germany
Dallas Museum of Art, Dallas, Texas
David Winton Bell Gallery, List Art Center, Brown University, Providence, Rhode Island
Denver Art Museum, Denver, Colorado
Des Moines Art Center, Des Moines, Iowa
Deutsche Bank, London
Dublin City Gallery The Hugh Lane, Dublin
DZ Bank AG Kunstsammlung, Frankfurt, Germany
Eastern Arts Association, Cambridge, England
Fine Arts Museum of San Francisco, de Young Museum, San Francisco
First Bank of Minneapolis, Minneapolis, Minnesota
Fogg Art Museum, Harvard University, Cambridge, Massachusetts
Foundation Stiftelsen Focus, Boras, Sweden
Ft. Lauderdale Museum of Art, Ft. Lauderdale, Florida
Fundació La Caixa, Barcelona
Fundación Allorda-Derksen, Barcelona
Fundación Bancaja, Valencia, Spain
Fundación Caixa Galicia, La Coruña, Spain
Fundación Grupo Urvasco (Homage to Chillida Collection), Vitoria-Gasteiz, Spain
Galleria d'Arte Moderna, Fondazione, Torino Musei
GAP Collection, San Francisco
Gemäldegalerie Neue Meister, Staatliche Kunstsammlungen Dresden, Dresden, Germany
Gertsev Collection, Moscow, Russia
High Museum of Art, Atlanta, Georgia
Hilti Art Foundation, Schaan, Liechtenstein
Hirshhorn Museum and Sculpture Garden, Washington, D.C.
Hood Museum of Art, Dartmouth College, Hanover, New Hampshire
Hôtel des Arts, Toulon, France
House of Fine Arts / Modern Gallery, László Vass Collection, Veszprém, Hungary
Hunterian Art Gallery, Glasgow, Scotland
Iris and B. Gerald Cantor Center for Visual Arts, Stanford University, Stanford, California
Irish Museum of Modern Art, Dublin
Institut Valencià d'Art Modern (IVAM), Valencia, Spain
Jean-Michel Cazes, Château Cordeillan-Bages, Pauillac, France
Kemper Museum of Contemporary Art, Kansas City, Missouri
Kunst und Museumsverein Wuppertal, Wuppertal, Germany
Kunsthalle Bielefeld, Bielefeld, Germany
Kunsthaus Zürich, Zürich

Kunstsammlung Nordrhein-Westfalen K20K21, Düsseldorf, Germany
La Colombe d'Or, St. Paul de Vence, France
La Fondation Edelman, Lausanne, Switzerland
Laing Art Gallery, Newcastle upon Tyne, England
Langen Foundation, Neuss, Germany
Leeum, Samsung Museum of Art, Seoul, Korea
Leicestershire Educational Authority, Leicester, England
Lentos Kunstmuseum Linz, Linz, Austria
Los Angeles County Museum of Art, Los Angeles, California
Louisiana Museum of Modern Art, Humlebæk, Denmark
Malaysian Exchange of Securities Dealing and Automated Quotation Collection, New York
Manchester City Art Gallery, Manchester, England
Maramotti Collection, Reggio Emilia, Italy
Maxine and Stuart Frankel Foundation for the Arts, Bloomfield Hills, Michigan
Mellon Bank, Pittsburgh, Pennsylvania
Metropolitan Museum of Art, New York
Miami Art Museum, Miami, Florida
Modern Art Museum of Fort Worth, Fort Worth, Texas
Mount Holyoke College Art Museum, South Hadley, Massachusetts
Musée d'Art Contemporain du Val-de Marne, Vitry-sur-Seine, France
Musée d'Art Moderne de Saint-Etienne Métropole, Saint-Etienne, France
Musée de Roland Garros, Paris
Musée du Dessin et de l'Estampe Originale, Gravelines, France
Musée Jenisch, Vevey, Switzerland
Musée National d'Art Moderne, Centre Georges Pompidou, Paris
Museo Chillida-Leku, Hernani, Spain
Museo de Arte Contemporaneo, Caracas, Venezuela
Museo de Arte Contemporaneo, Monterrey, Mexico
Museo de Arte Moderna di Bologna, Bologna, Italy
Museo de Arte Moderno, Col. Bosques de Chapultepec, Mexico
Museo de Arte Moderno, Mexico City, Mexico
Museo Nacional Centro de Arte Reina Sofia, Madrid
Museu d'Art Contemporani de Barcelona, Barcelona
Museu de Montserrat, Abadia de Montserrat, Barcelona
Museum Folkwang, Essen, Germany
Museum Moderner Kunst, Vienna, Austria
Museum of Fine Arts, Boston, Massachusetts
Museum of Fine Arts, Houston, Texas
Museum of Modern Art, New York
Museum Pfalzgalerie, Kaiserslautern, Germany
Nagoya City Art Museum, Nagoya, Japan
National Gallery of Art, Washington, D.C.

National Gallery of Australia, Canberra, Australia
National Gallery of Victoria, Melbourne, Australia
National Museum Cardiff, Cardiff, Wales
Neue Galerie, Museumlandschaft Hessen, Kassel, Germany
Neue Pinakothek, Bayerische Staatsgemäldesammlung, Munich, Germany
Newsweek, New York
Northern Arts Association, Newcastle upon Tyne, England
Norwich Castle Museum, Norwich, England
Open Museum, Environmental & Heritage Resource Centre, Leicestershire, England
Orlando Museum of Art, Orlando, Florida
Paine Webber Group, Inc., New York
Philadelphia Museum of Art, Pennsylvania
Philip Morris, Inc., New York
Phillips Collection, Washington, D.C.
Pier Arts Centre, Orkney, Scotland
Power Institute, University of Sydney, Sydney, Australia
Princeton University Art Museum, Princeton, New Jersey
Reader's Digest Art Collection, New York
Rose Art Museum, Brandeis University, Waltham, Massachusetts
Ruhr Universitat, Bochum, Germany
Saastamoisen Säätiö, Helsinki, Finland
Saint Louis Art Museum, Saint Louis, Missouri
Sala Rekalde, Bilbao, Spain
Sammlung Essl, Vienna / Klosterneuburg, Austria
Sammlung Ströher, Darmstadt, Germany
San Diego Museum of Art, San Diego, California
Santa Barbara Museum of Art, Santa Barbara, California
Sara Hilden Art Museum, Tampere, Finland
Seattle Art Museum, Seattle, Washington
Shearson Lehman American Express Inc., New York
Sheldon Memorial Art Gallery and Sculpture Garden, University of Nebraska, Lincoln, Nebraska
Smith College Museum of Art, Northampton, Massachusetts
Smithsonian American Art Museum, Washington, D.C.
Snite Museum of Art, Notre Dame, Indiana
Solomon R. Guggenheim Museum, New York
Staatliche Graphische Sammlung München, Munich, Germany
Staatliche Kunstsammlungen Dresden, Dresden, Germany
Staatliche Museen Kassel, Neue Galerie, Kassel, Germany
Staatsgalerie, Stuttgart, Germany
Städel Museum, Städelsches Kunstinstitut und Städtische Galerie, Frankfurt am Main, Germany
Städtische Galerie im Lenbachhaus, Munich, Germany
Strasbourg Museum of Modern and Contemporary Art, Strasbourg, France

Tate Gallery, London
Tehran Museum of Contemporary Art, Tehran, Iran
Tel Aviv Museum of Art, Tel Aviv, Israel
Tokyo International Forum Art Collection, Tokyo
UBS Art Collection, New York and Zürich
UCLA Grunwald Center for the Graphic Arts / Hammer Museum, Los Angeles, California
Ulster Museum, Belfast, Northern Ireland
University of Limerick, Limerick, Ireland
University of Northumbria, Newcastle, England
Van Cliburn Foundation, Fort Worth, Texas
Victoria and Albert Museum, London
Virginia Museum of Fine Arts, Richmond, Virginia
Von der Heydt Museum, Wuppertal, Germany
Wadsworth Atheneum Museum of Art, Hartford, Connecticut
Walker Art Center, Minneapolis, Minnesota
Whitney Museum of American Art, New York
Whitworth Art Gallery, Manchester, England
Wilhelm-Hack-Museum, Ludwigshafen am Rhein, Germany
Willy Michel Collection, Museum Franz Gertsch, Burgdorf, Switzerland
Yale University Art Gallery, New Haven, Connecticut
Zentrum für Kunst und Medientechnologie, Karlsruhe, Germany

Dust jacket, front cover: *Stack 5.5.16*, 2016, watercolor on paper, 30 1/4 × 22 in, 76.8 × 55.9 cm. Dust jacket, back cover: *Wall of Light Cubed 9.20.15*, 2015, oilstick on paper, 22 × 30 1/4 in, 55.9 × 76.8 cm (per sheet). Cover: *Wall of Light Cubed 9.20.15*, 2015 (detail). Frontispiece: *Landline Cubed*, 2015, graphite on paper, 11 × 8 1/2 in, 27.9 × 21.6 cm. Page 44, *Untitled Tower*, 1982, graphite on paper, 14 × 11 in, 35.6 × 27.9 cm. Pages 50-51, *Wall of Light Cubed*, 2007, ink on paper, 11 × 8 1/2 in, 27.9 × 21.6 cm (each). Portrait: Liliane Tomasko. Printed in Italy by Trifolio. Photography Robert Bean, Brian Buckley, Francois Deladerriere, Frank Hutter, and Josh Kessler. ISBN 978-1-944316-07-5. Images of all artworks © Sean Scully.

SEAN SCULLY

Design John Cheim

Essay Pac Pobric

Editor Ellen Robinson

Special thanks to Adam Sheffer

Published on the occasion of the 2017 Cheim & Read exhibition